Clean Water

Saving Our Planet

This is **clean water.**

We all need clean water.

Look at the bird.
The bird can find food
in clean water.

Look at the shark.

The shark can find food in clean water.

The kangaroo likes the clean water.

Look at the **flowers.**
The flowers can grow
in clean water.

I can help to keep the water clean.

clean water

flowers